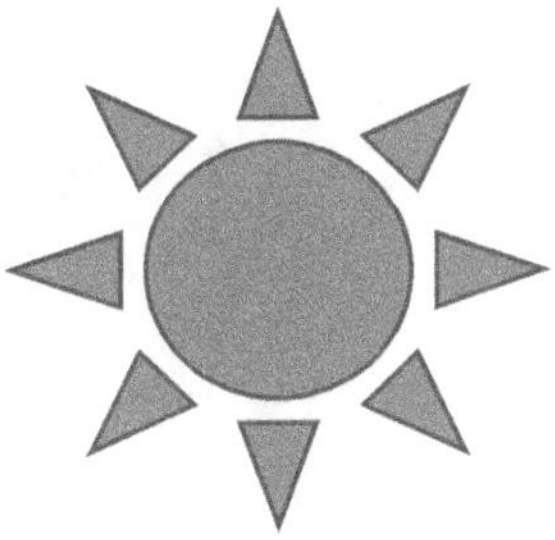

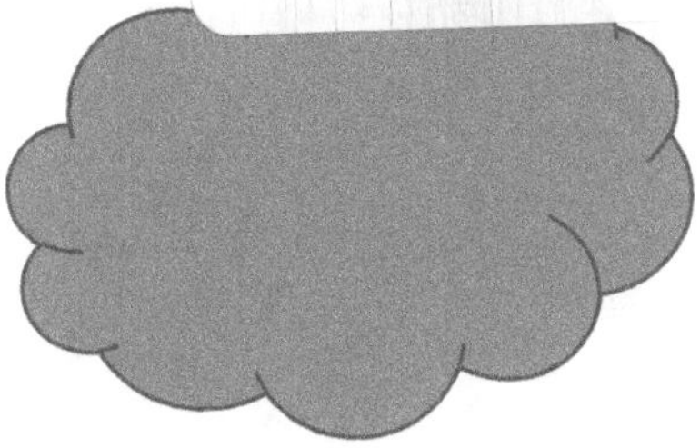

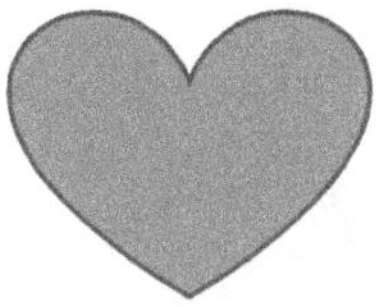

COLORING BOOKS FOR TODDLERS

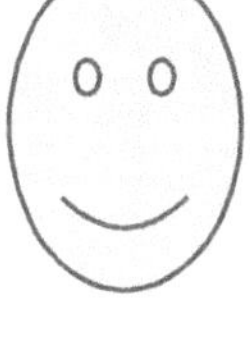

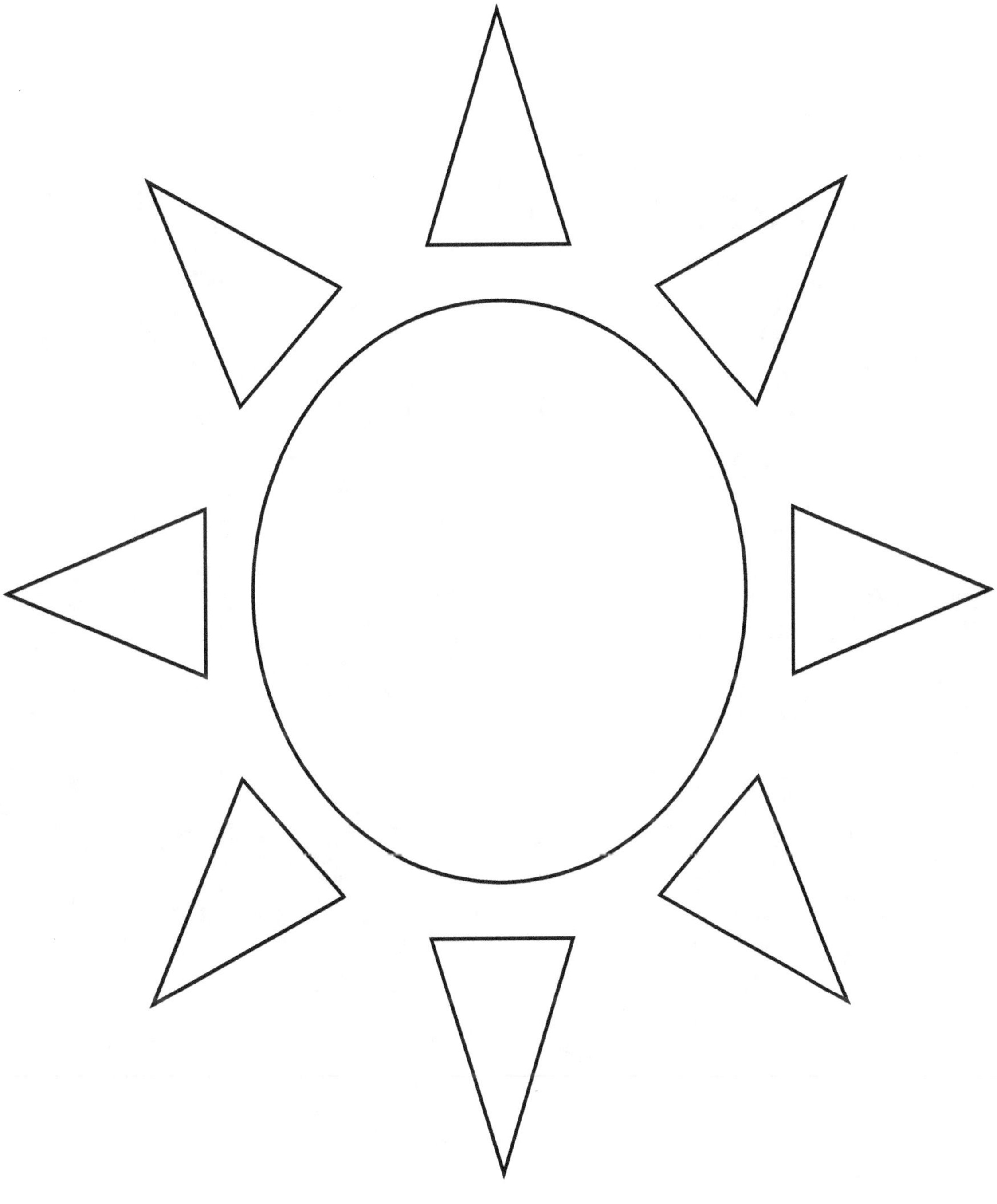

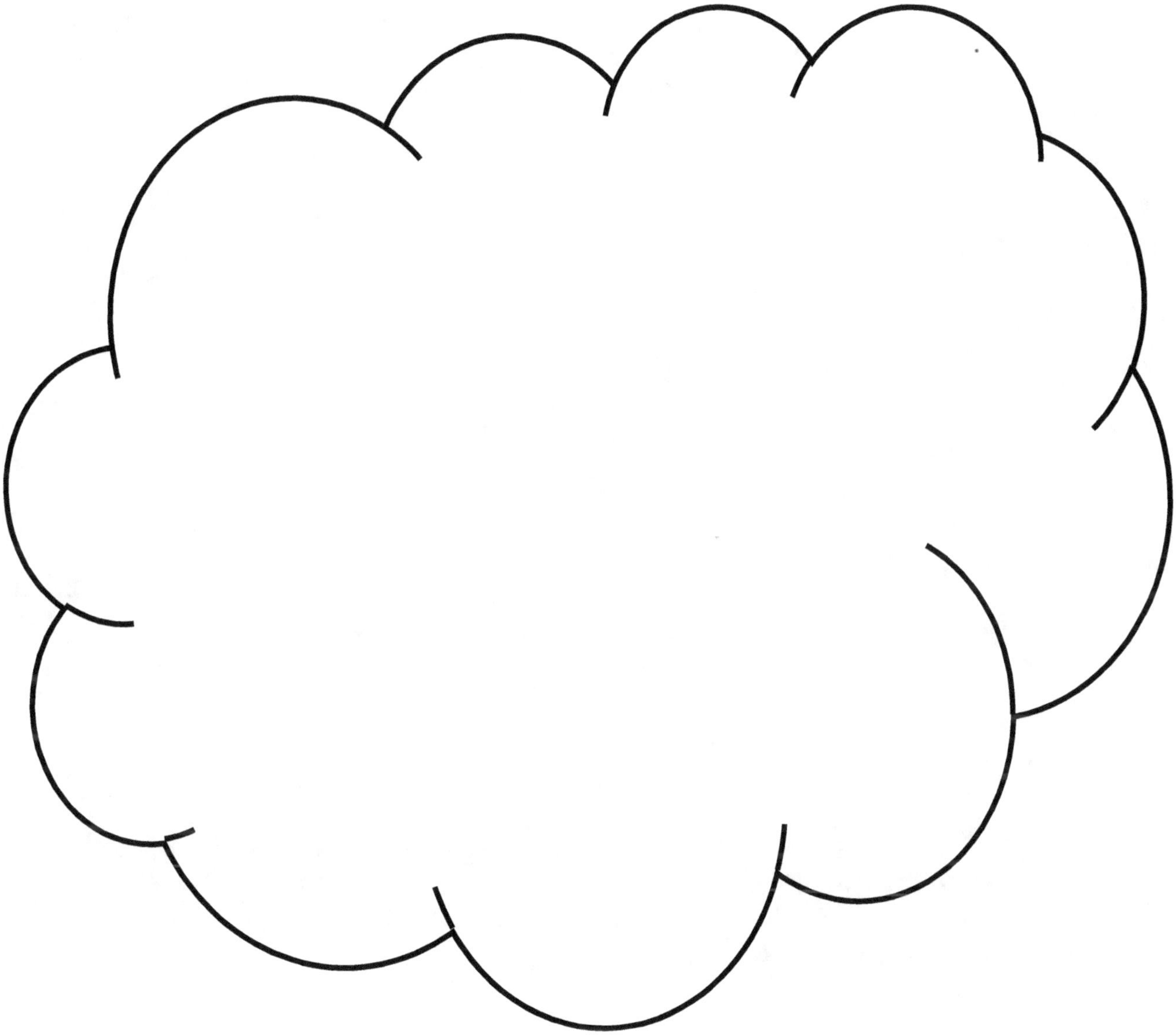

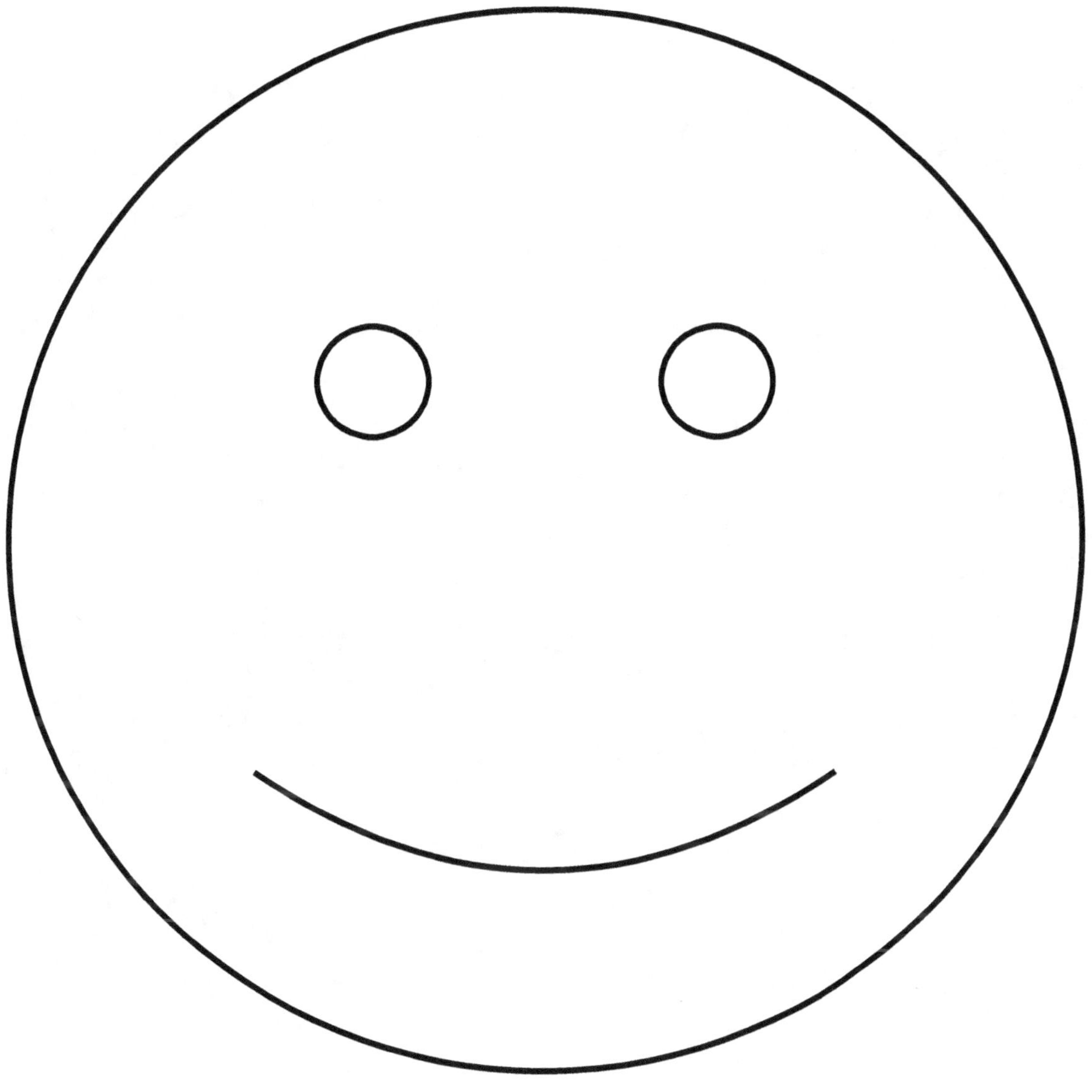

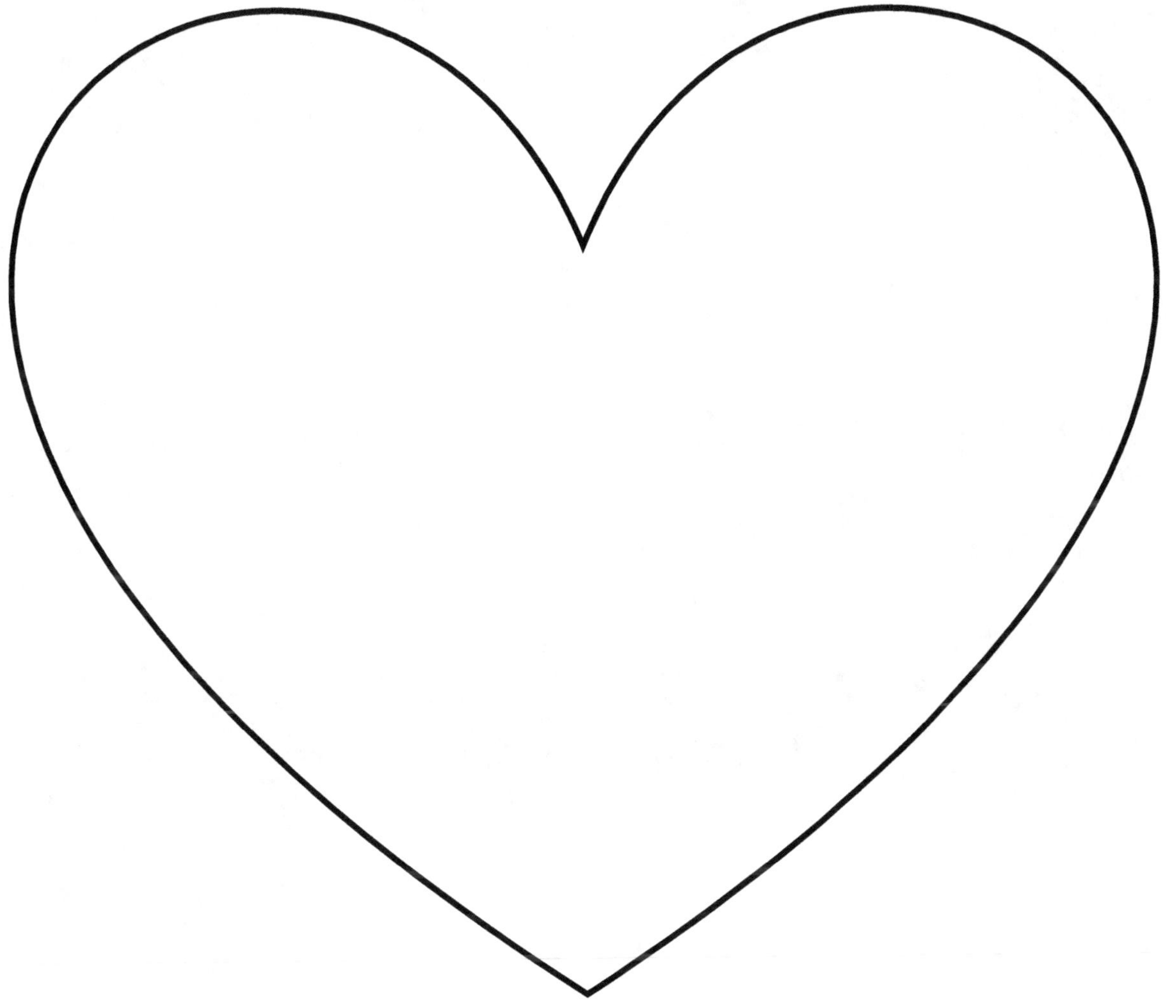

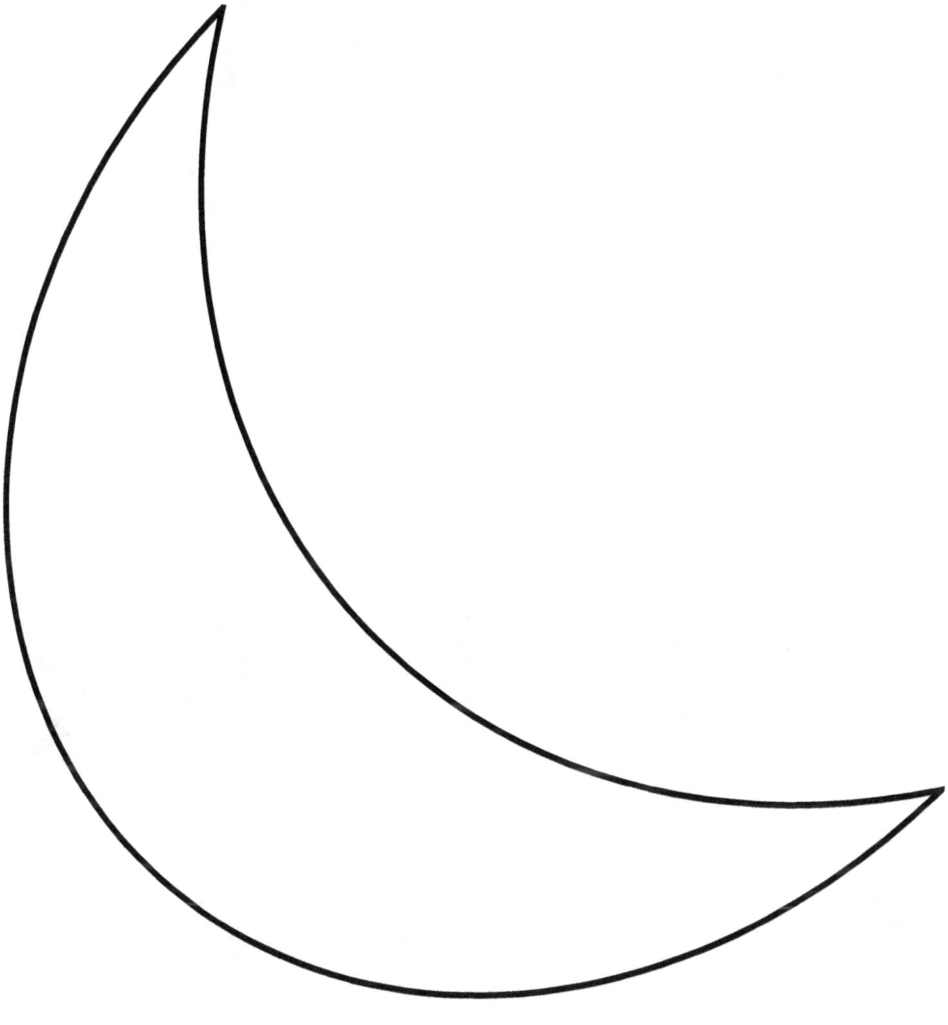

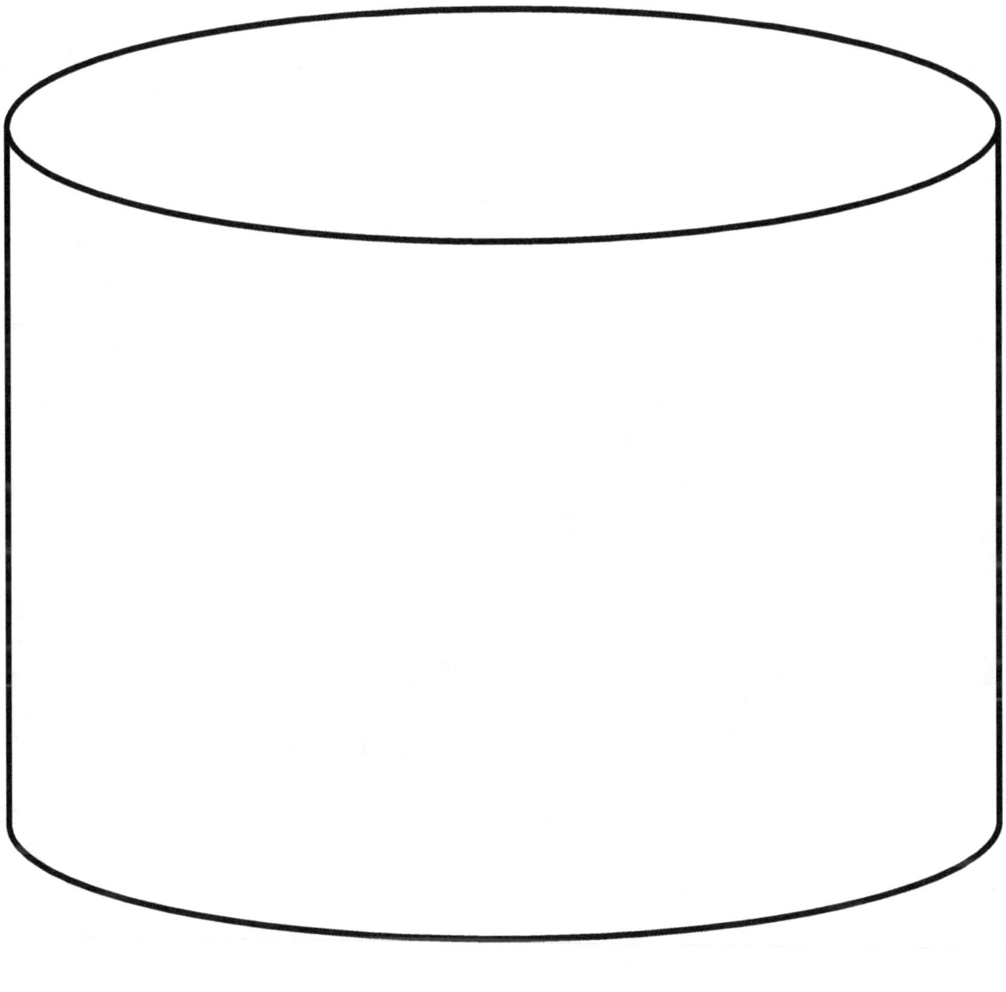

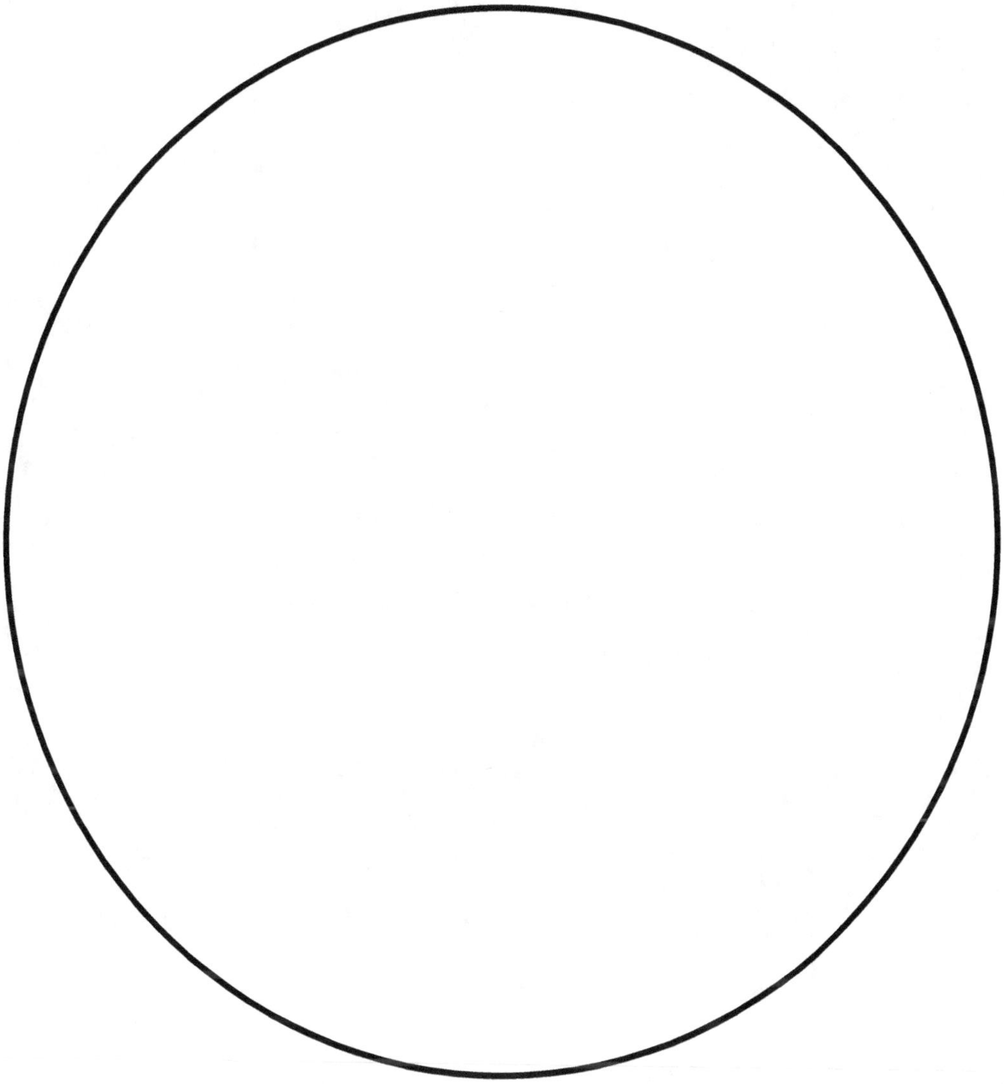

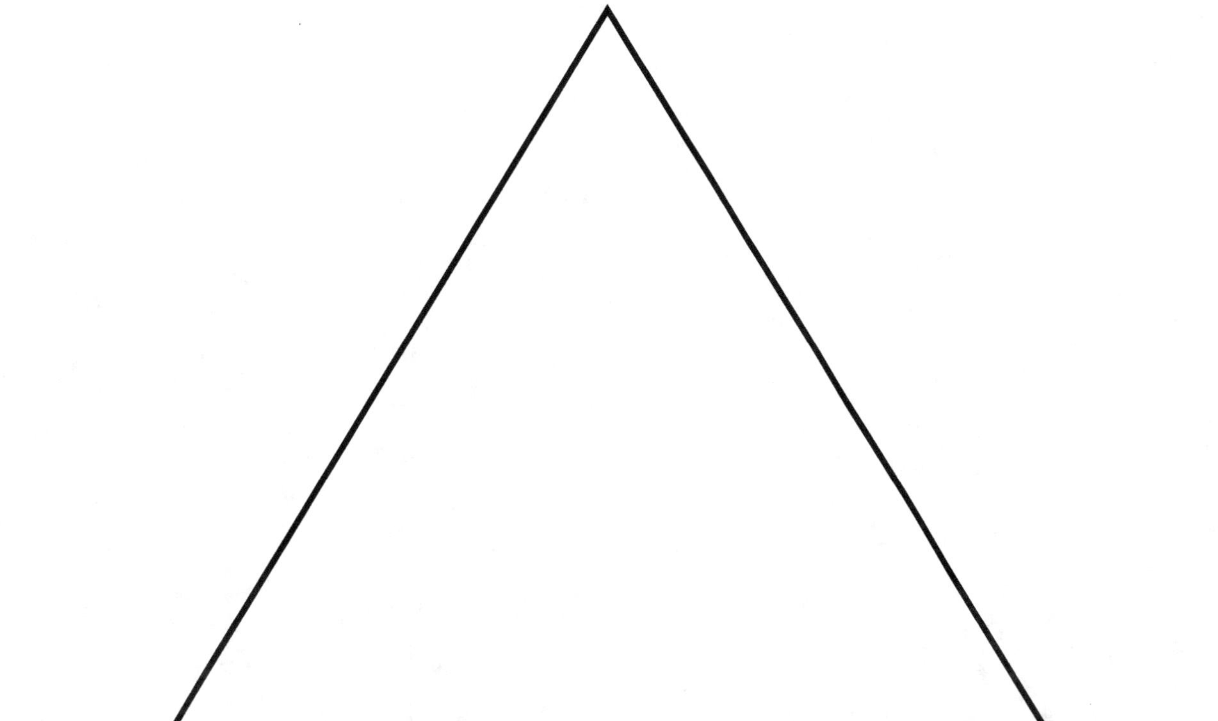

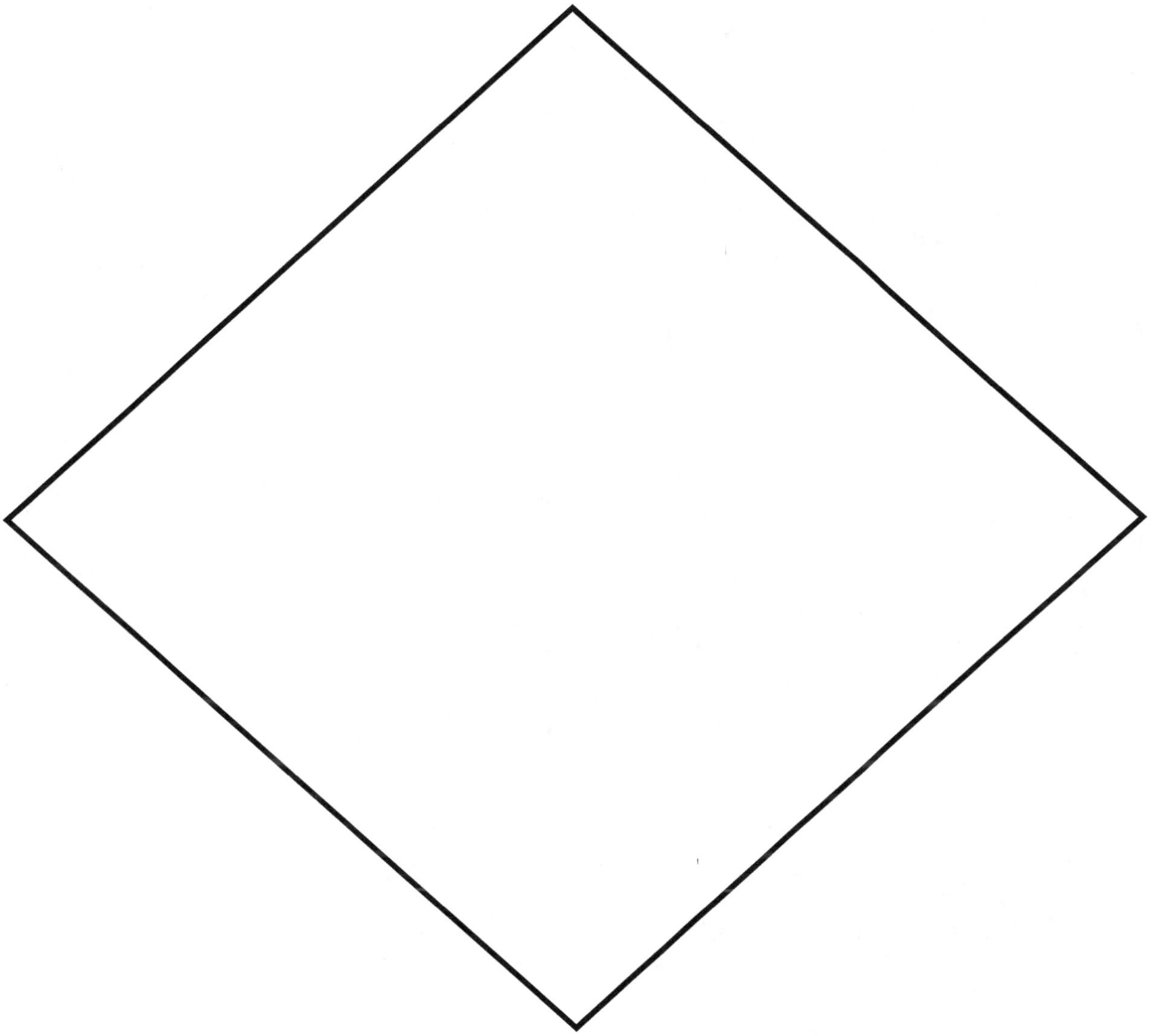

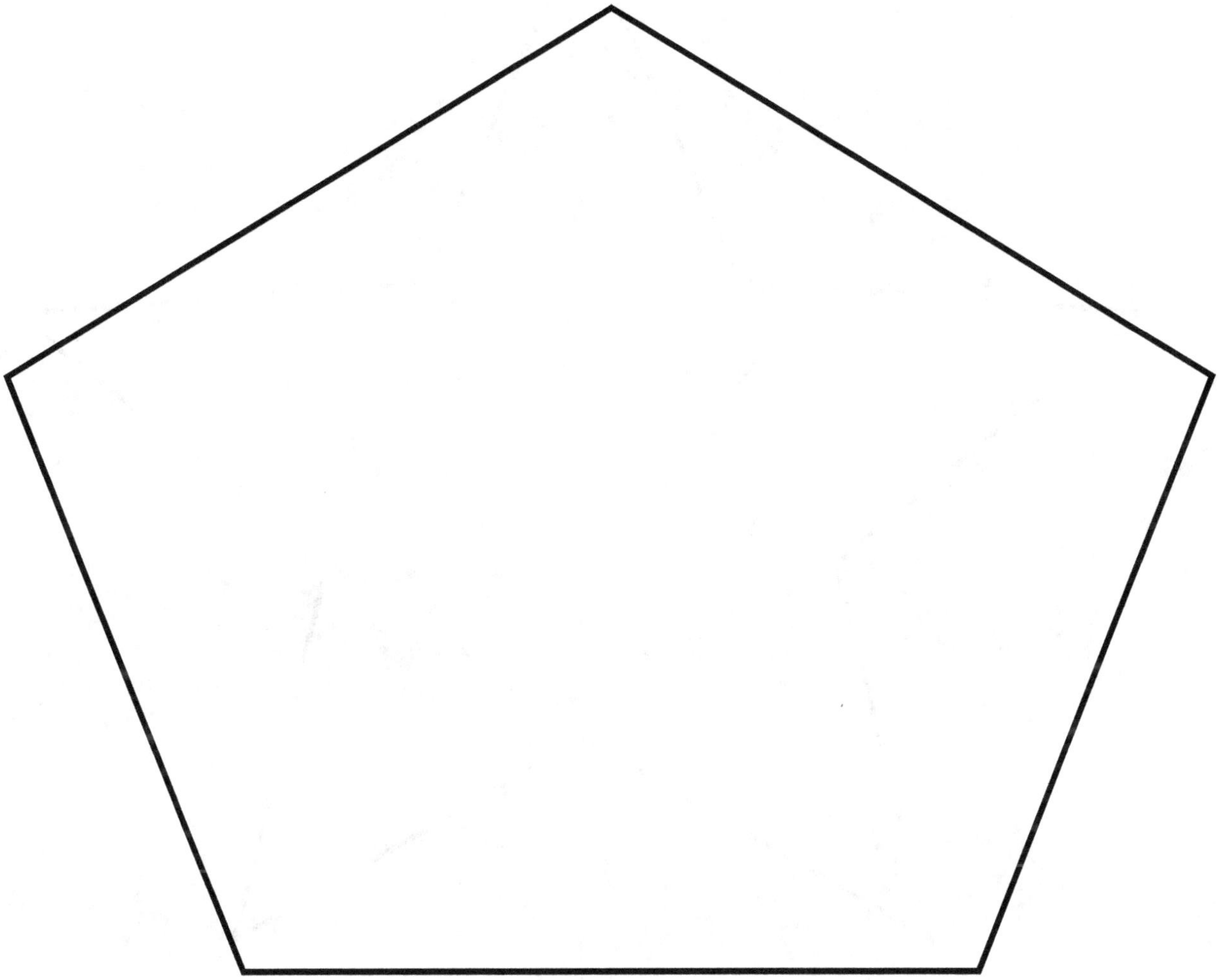

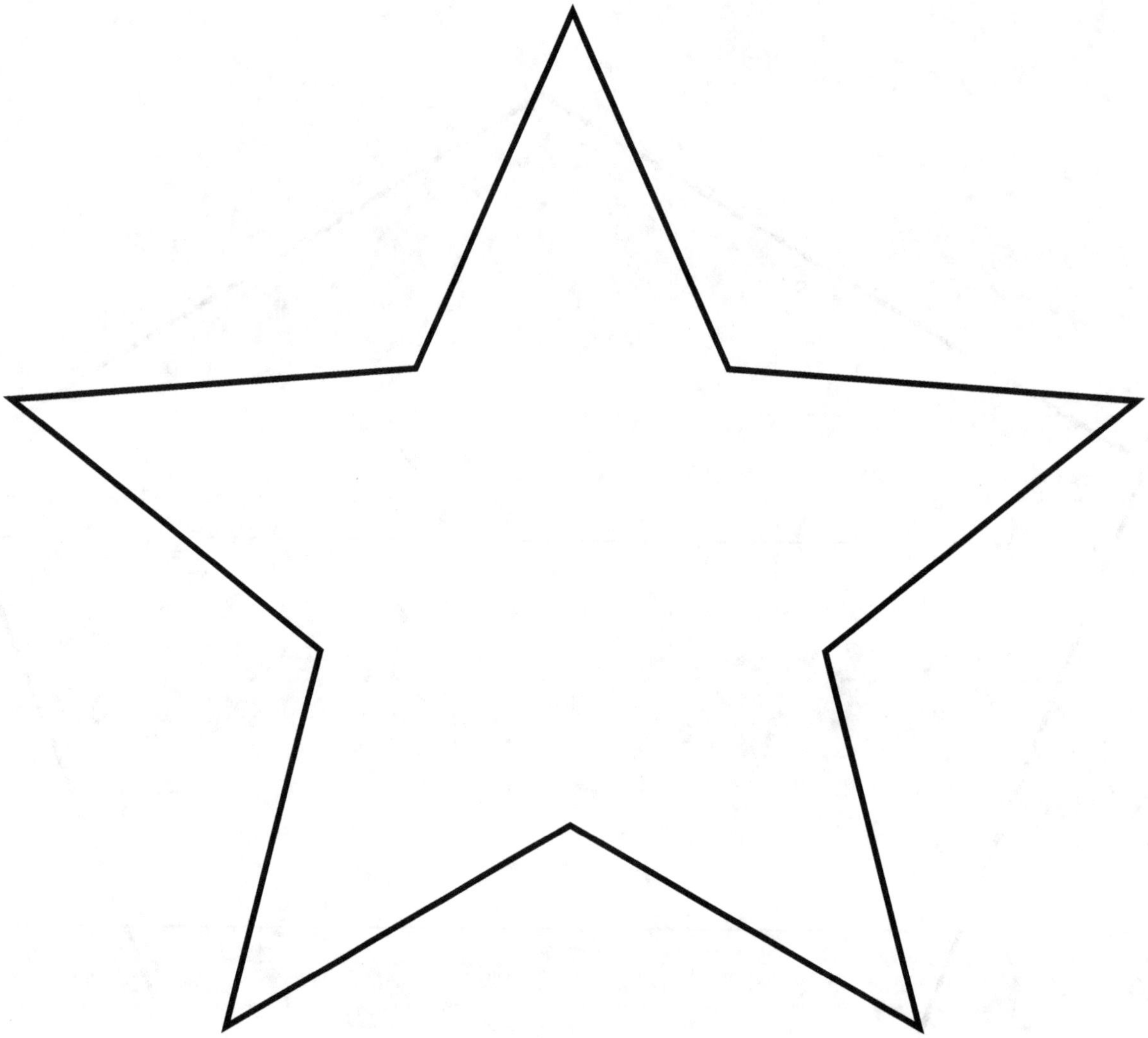

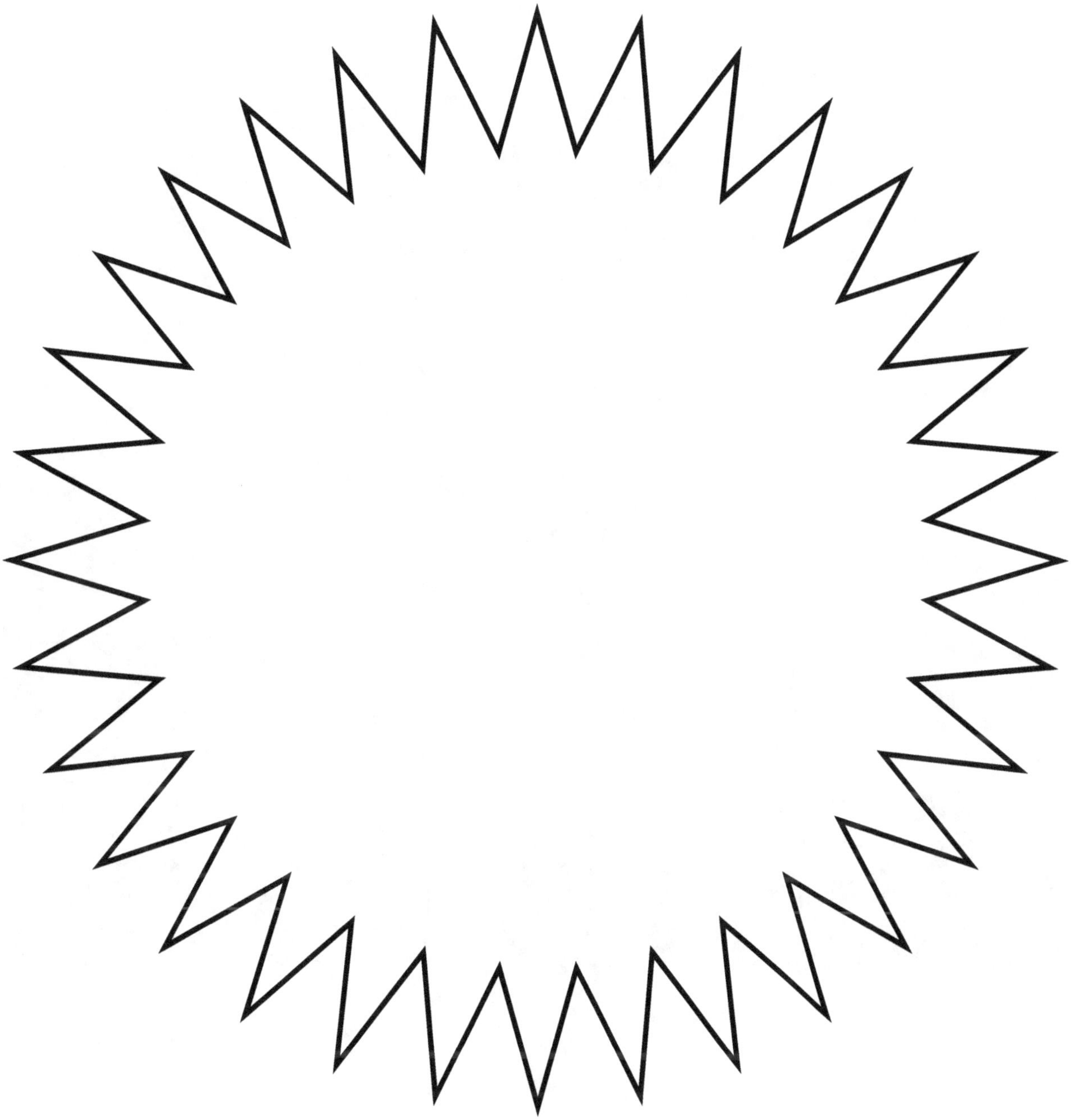

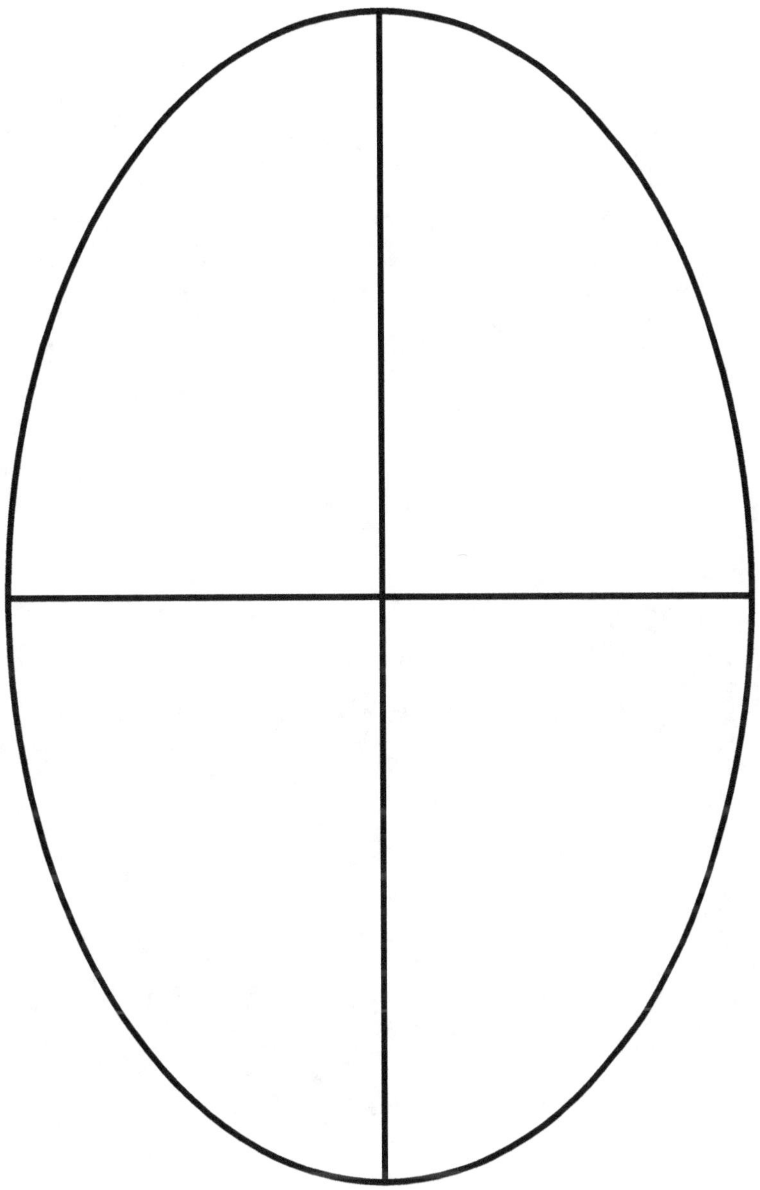

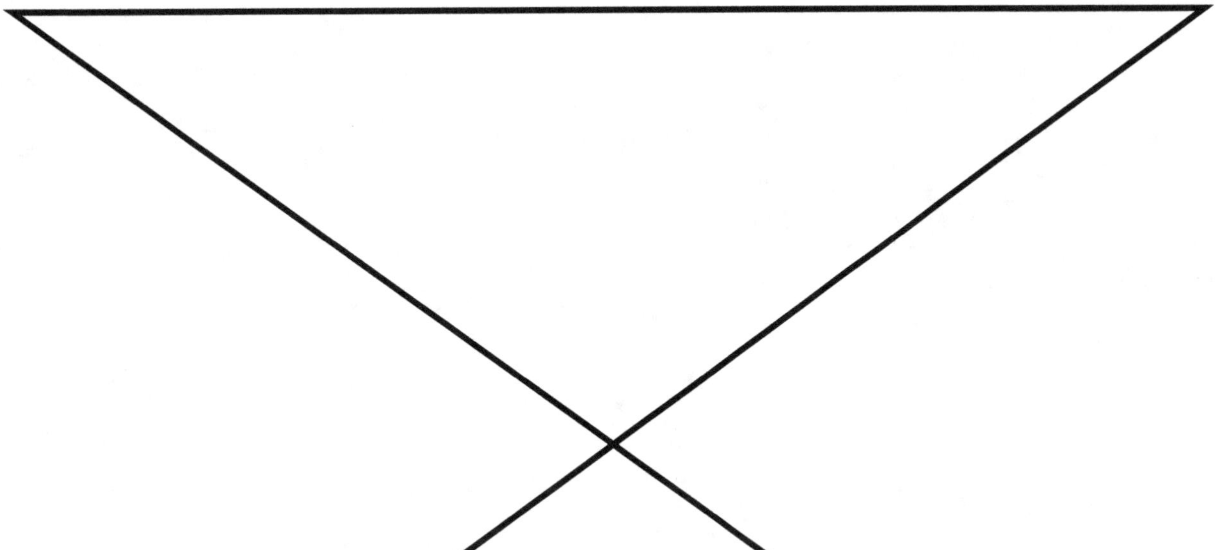

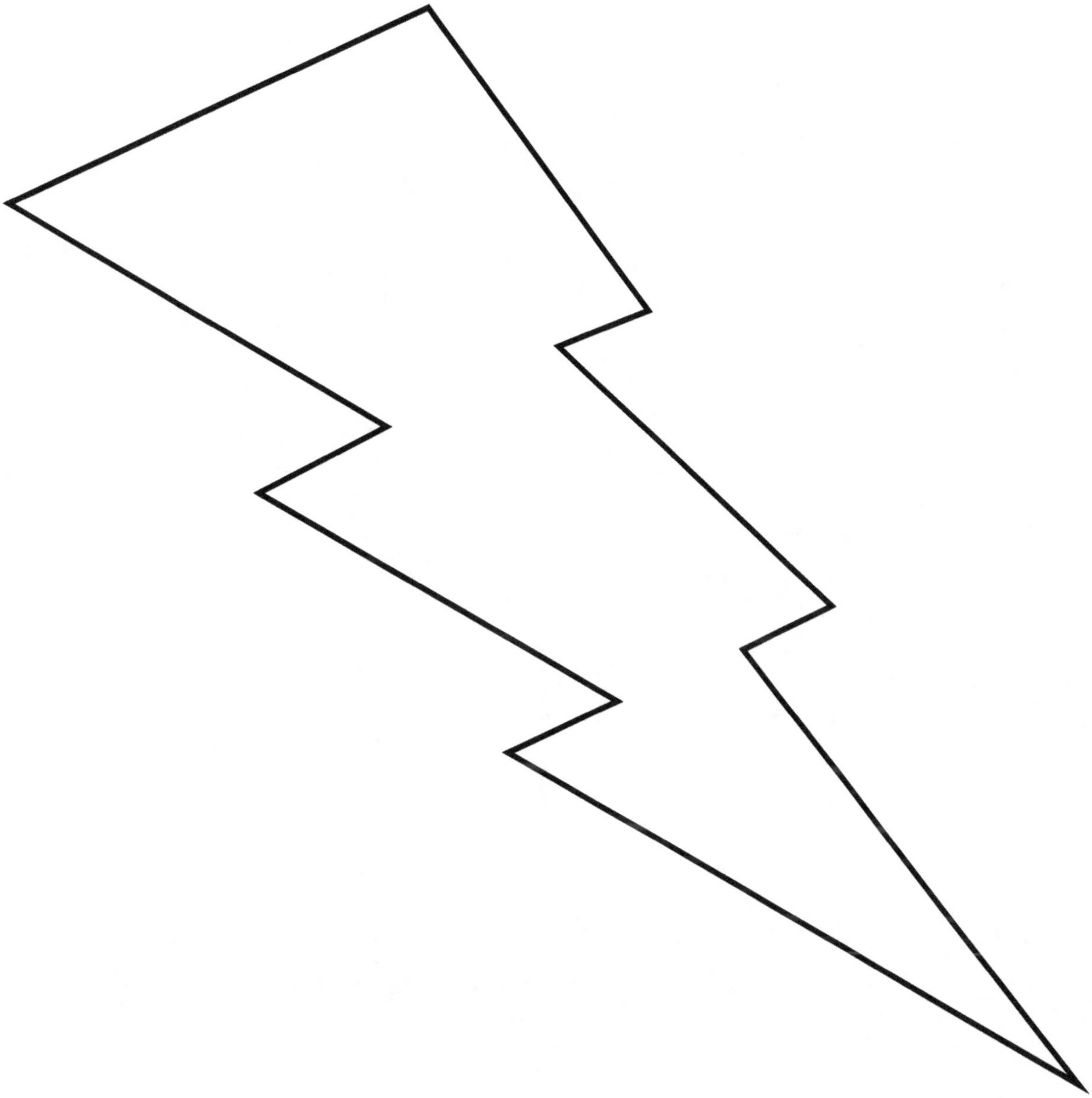

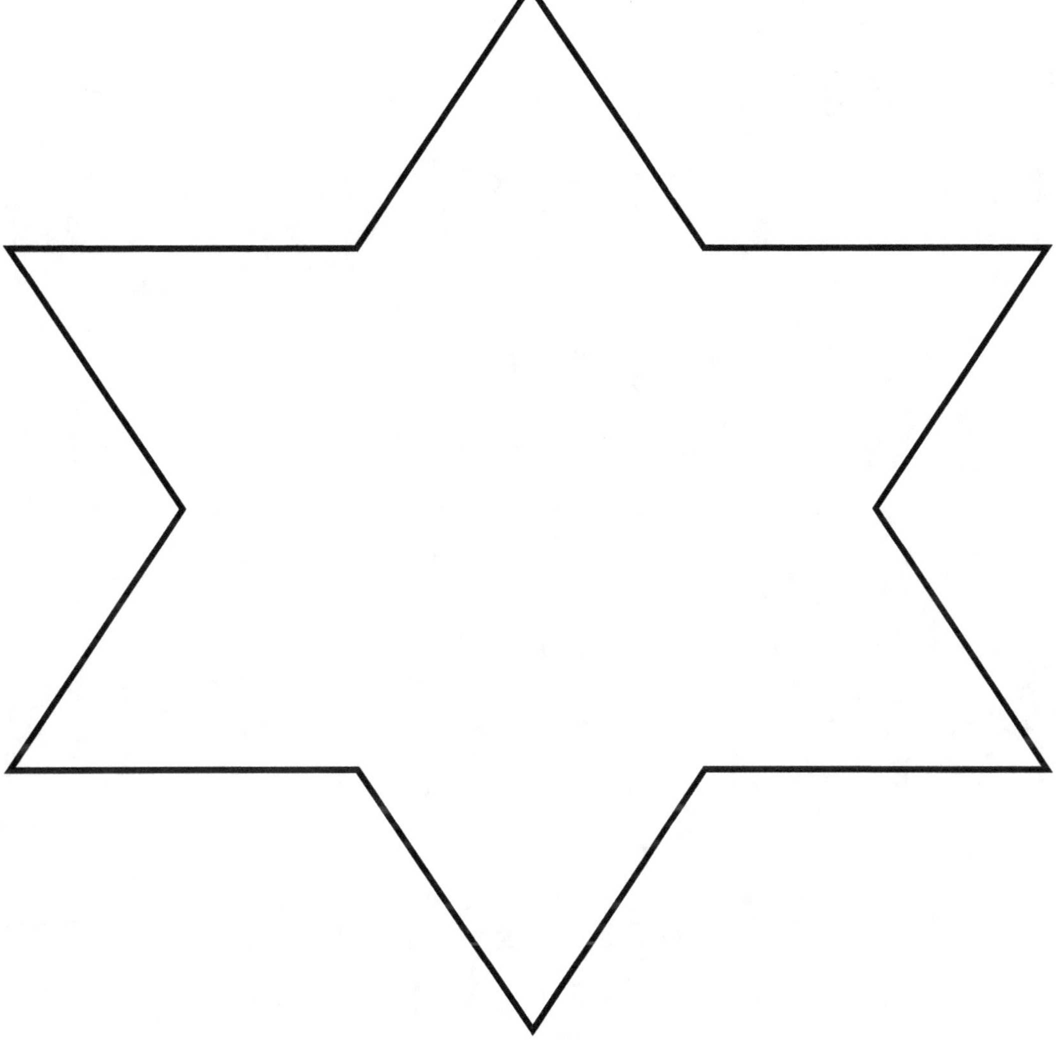

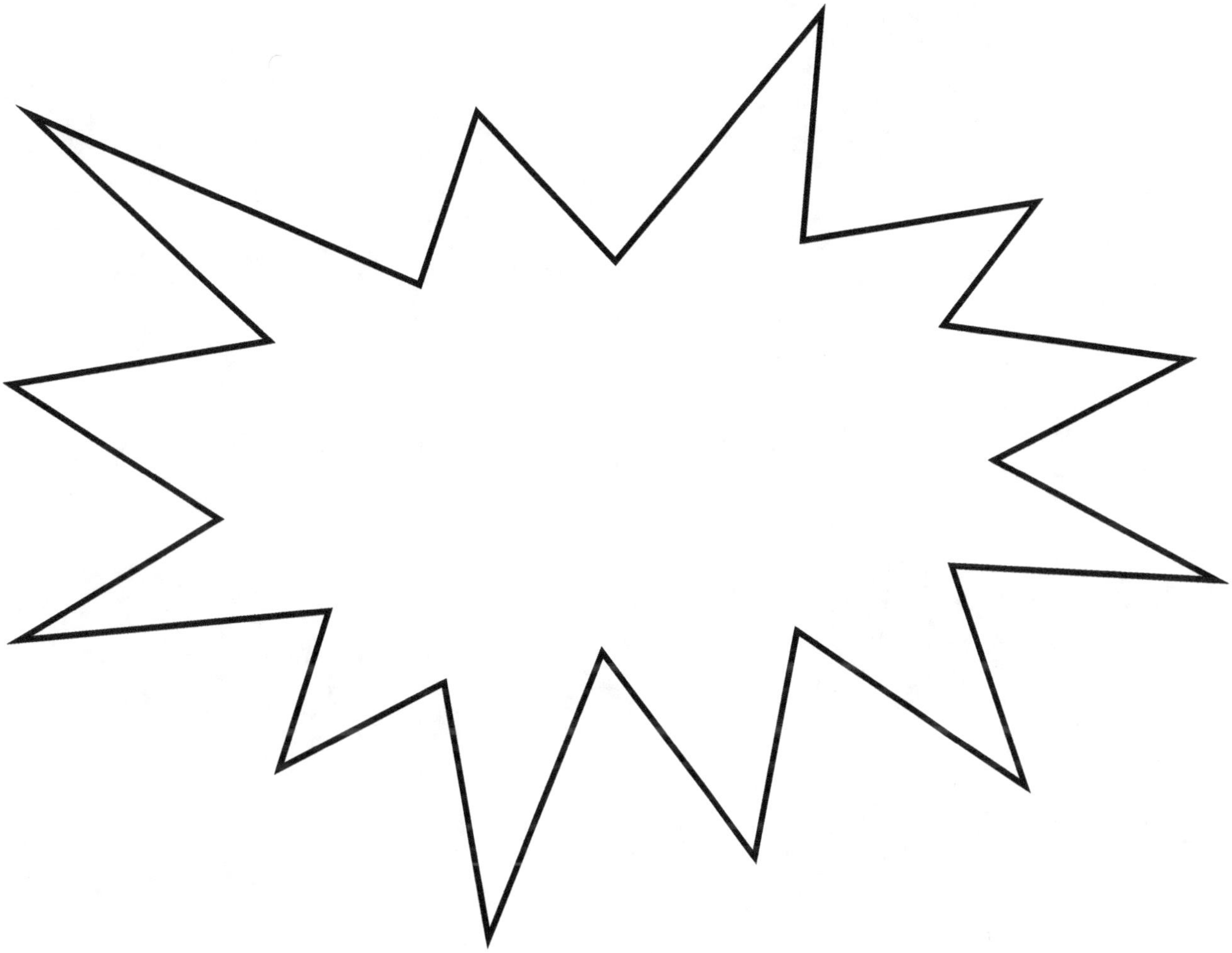

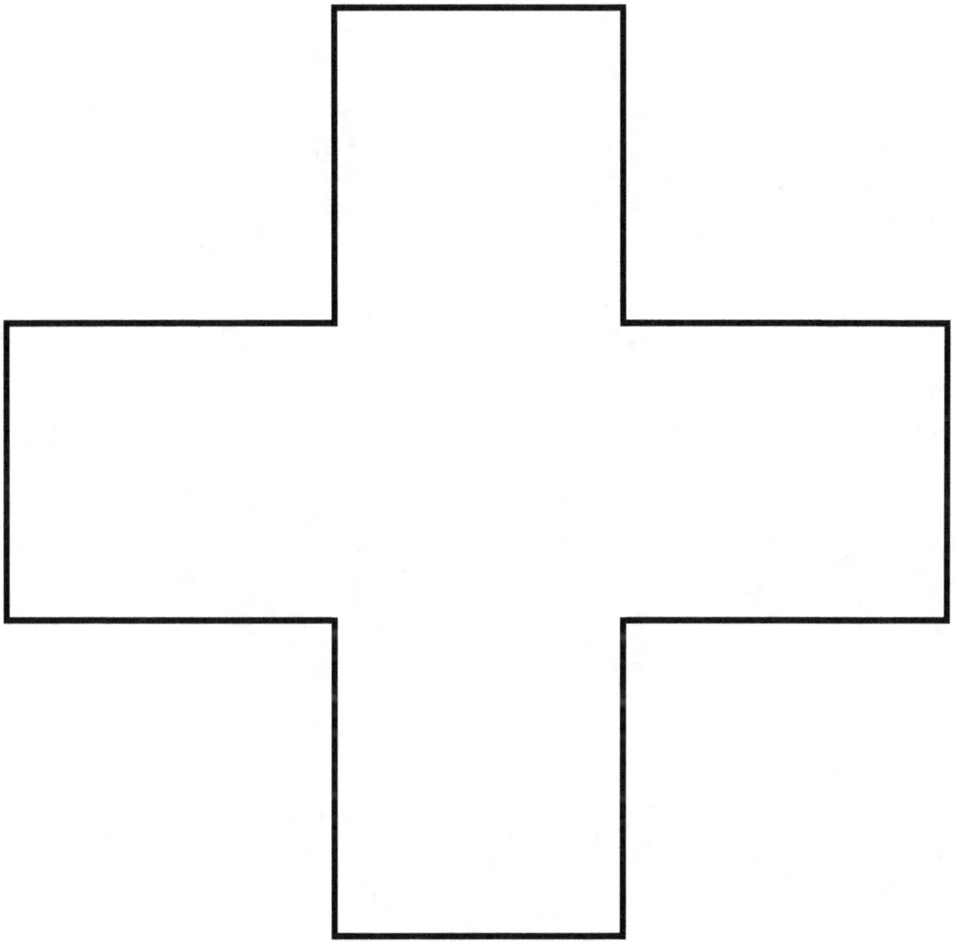

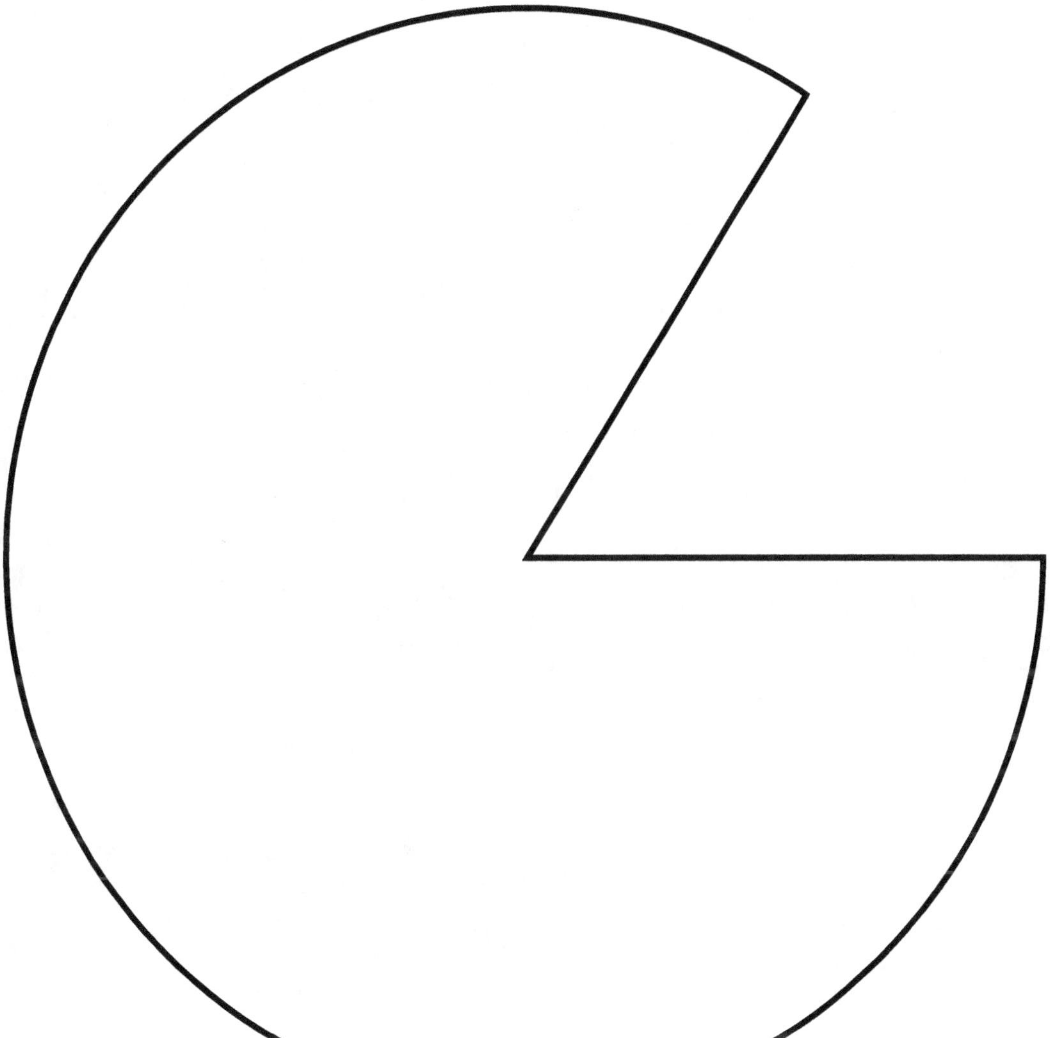

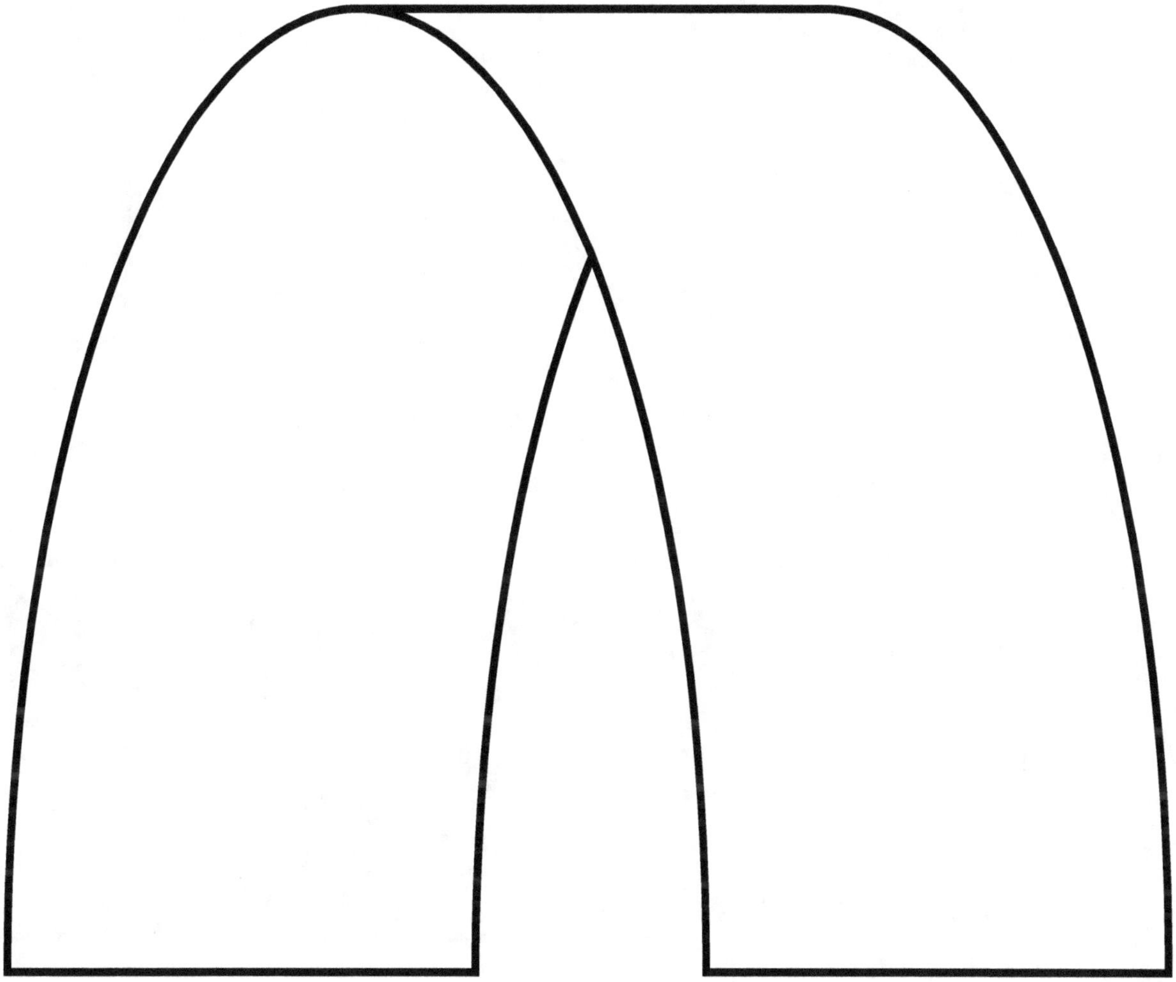

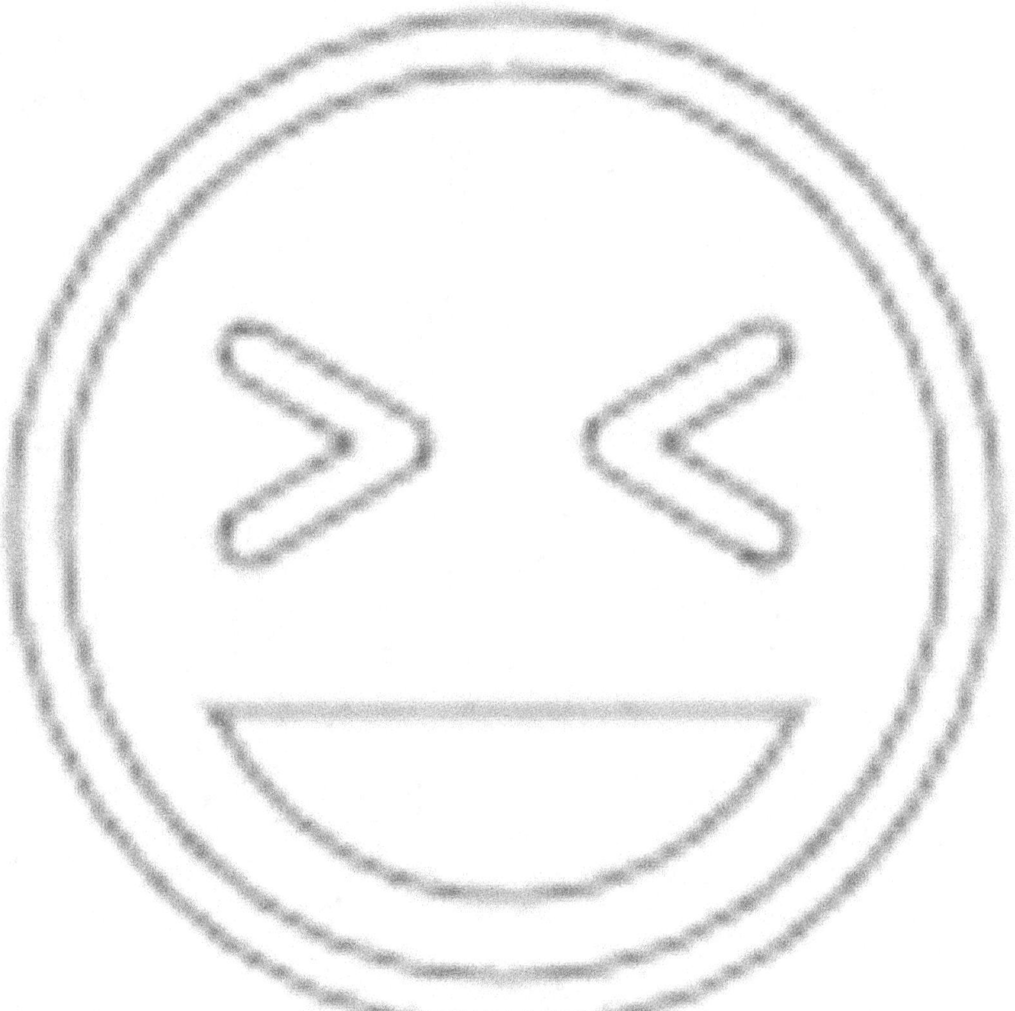

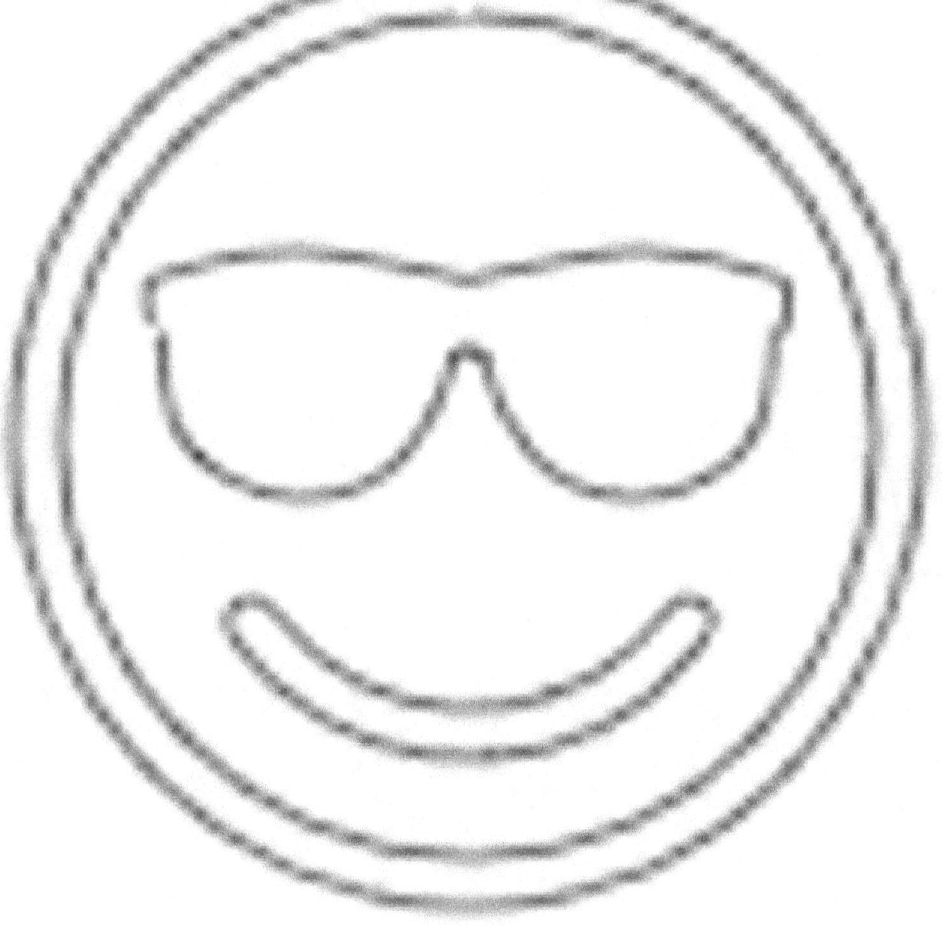

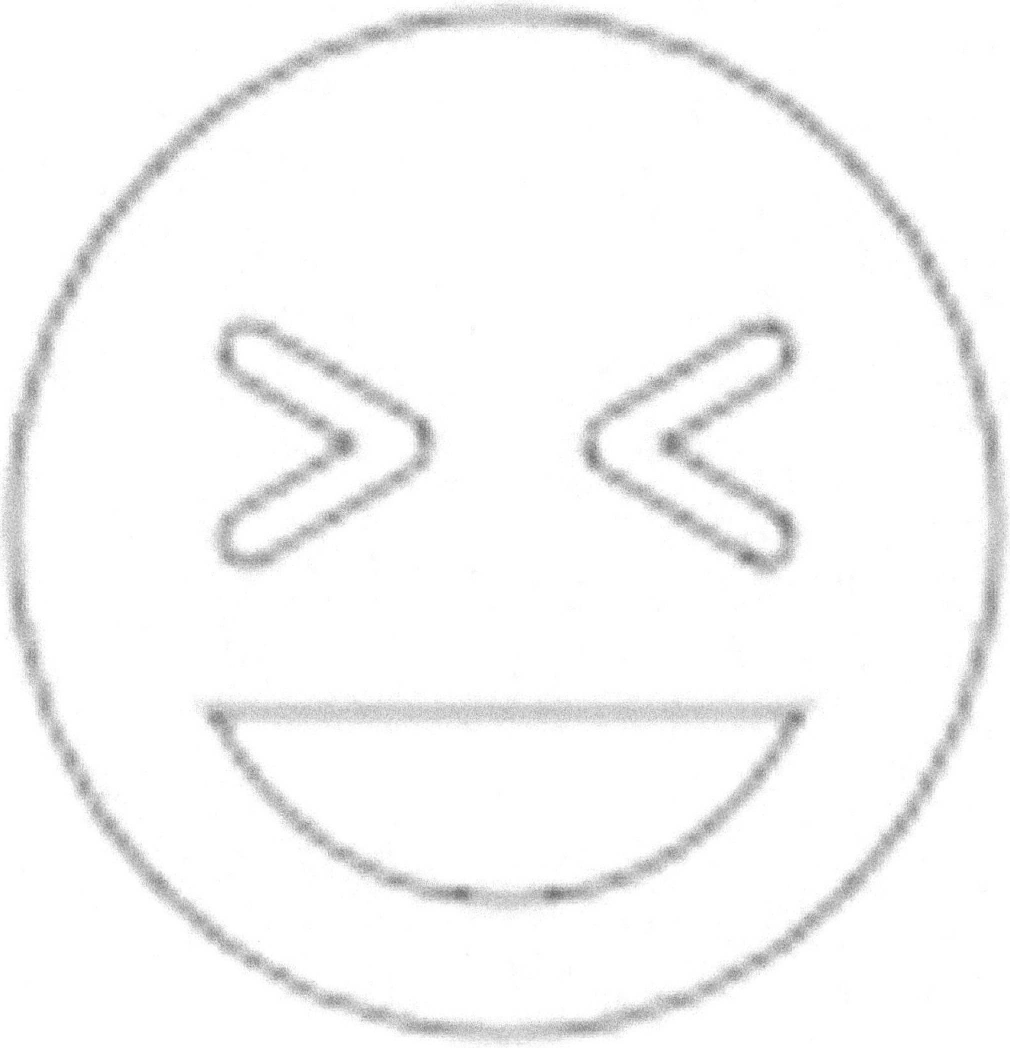

www.ingramcontent.com/pod-product-compliance
Lightning Source LLC
Chambersburg PA
CBHW080846170526
45158CB00009B/2645
* 9 7 8 1 0 8 0 5 3 1 7 7 6 *